Character — What is it Anyway?

It can be your best friend or your worst enemy.

2nd Edition—With Study Guide

D. Daniel Jones

YAV Publications

Asheville, North Carolina

ISBN 978-0-9790221-6-6

Unless otherwise noted, Scripture quotations are taken from *The King James Version* of the Holy Bible.

Published by:

YAV Publications

Asheville, North Carolina

YAV books may be purchased in bulk for educational, business, fund-raising, or sales promotional use.
For information, please contact Books@yav.com
Visit our website: www.InterestingWriting.com
See last page for author's contact information.

3 5 7 9 10 8 6 4

Assembled in the United States of America

Published April 2011

ENDORSEMENTS

This book approaches the topic of 'character' in a unique way. The generous use of scriptures and the straightforward dealing with the subject matter is refreshing and challenging. I strongly recommend this book for every minister and layperson alike. The principles are the same for all church people, and Dan Jones has clearly delineated the path of character for all to follow. I thoroughly enjoyed this book for its practicality and Biblically based content.

Douglas E. Fulenwider
District Superintendent
Louisiana District Council of the Assemblies of God
Alexandria, LA

One of my first reactions upon reading Dan's book, *Character, What Is It Anyway?* was, "This is good stuff!" I love it. It touches upon every point of character. The book should be in every church, school and bookstore. Everyone would benefit from reading this book.

Pastor Thurman Scrivner
The Living Savior Ministries
Justin, Texas, U.S.A. TLSM.org

Dan's book *Character, What Is It Anyway?* is not a book to put down when you start reading it. When I read the manuscript, I felt this may be the only book of its kind, which hits straight to the core of what character is and then defining it specifically. It is a kind of handbook, a kind of reference point to help us evaluate our character, and keep us on track. I have made up my mind to use the book as a discipleship-training course for all my church members and a course to be taught to all our students in our Bible School and Seminary. Thank you, Dan, for yielding yourself to the Holy Spirit to be used for such a great project.

Rev. Chuks Ihim.
Former Executive Director,
Focus on the Family, Nigeria.
Pastor, Family Helps Gospel
Church, Abuja, Nigeria

Dan's book on character is one that will challenge the reader to examine the role character plays and has played in his life. This book, *Character, What Is It Anyway?* shows us what character actually is and how we can strengthen our character for the betterment of our lives, and others. The book is straight and direct, makes good use of scriptures, and is worthy of publication. The element of character is an underlying factor in every society. You may choose to disagree with Dan on the strong approach he takes at times to point us in the right direction, but his passion is to bring us to a place of strengthening this precious jewel (character) that will enhance our lives here and for eternity. From time to time we need to be awakened, stirred by the heart of another, to be able to see all the potential within us.

Pastor Terrence Sisneros
Destiny Church
San Antonio, Texas, U.S.A.

Acknowledgements

At first, I had no intention of writing this book. Instead, I was inspired to write a tract. However, as I was writing the tract, a thought came to me that I never had before, that had to do with character. I liked it. So I plugged it into the tract. Then later another thought I likewise never had had before came to me, and I plugged it into the tract too. Similarly, more and more thoughts came about character that were not mine—many of them, sometimes day after day; and I soon realized these thoughts were not coming from me; they were coming from Him. For example, I had no idea that there are over forty character traits. (God was teaching me as I was writing). Then one day my Editor friend, Chris Yavelow, said in words to the effect, "That's not a tract. It's become a book." I now know without a doubt that most of the material in this book—if not all of it—came from the Holy Spirit; and I give Him all the credit for writing it. In fact, my son's father in-law, after reading this book, could hardly believe I wrote it. He asked me, "Dan, did you have a ghost writer?" I said, "Yes, the Holy Ghost."

I would like to express my appreciation to my Editor and friend, Christopher Yavelow, at YAV Publications. With his encyclopedic knowledge, professionalism, and many years of experience in the publishing arena he has been of enormous help to me in the editing of this book, and guiding me through the publication process. Chris is also a Publisher and an Author. Thank you Chris.

This book is dedicated to my sons Peter and Richard and their families.

In loving memory of my wife Isabel.

Table of Contents

For the sake of simplicity, I have chosen to use the masculine pronouns (he, his, him, himself), although it refers equally to both men and women.

Chapter 1

This Elusive Subject of Character

Everyone knows what salt tastes like, but can anyone describe its taste? Likewise, we all know what character is. Yet, I have never heard of a specific definition of character. The definition of character is elusive, and the subject has received little attention—even though it is of paramount importance to the human race.

Dictionaries, psychologists, teachers, and others "define" character by mentioning some character traits such as persistence, patience, moral strength, and so forth. However, these traits in and of themselves, are not character. Rather, the traits are descriptions of character, and are not definitions of character. We know much about character, by being familiar with its many traits. However, we have not answered the question: *What is character?* I thought long and hard about this for months; and eventually the specific definition of character just popped into my head. This, I provide towards the end of the book. In fact, the subject of character is so vast and so deep that no brief description will do, as I will show.

Some people have great character. Some have weak character. Some are devoid of character. Why is that? Why do people have different levels of character? Character is vital. But where does character come from? Is character inherited? Is it acquired? How do we get it? How can we strengthen our character? And what is character anyway?

Character is usually "defined" or referred to in nebulous terms. I propose to show specifically what character is, how we can identify character, how we acquire character, and how we can strengthen our character. This will lead to a proper definition of character.

Whenever a hard truth is presented it can be offensive and even painful. However, "no pain, no gain." The late Latin bandleader, Xavier Cugat, once said in words to the effect that, "He who tells me of my faults is my friend. He who flatters me is my enemy." There is much truth to that statement. *A flattering mouth worketh ruin.* (Proverbs 26:28). So I hope you regard me as your friend, even though you may be offended at what I have to say. It is my wish that you profit from reading these words, because any criticism is meant to be constructive criticism.

First, an example:

Before I demonstrate what character is, how we get character, and how we can strengthen character, I first want to recount a true story about a butterfly. You may have heard it before.

A man noticed a butterfly on his windowsill, struggling to get out of its cocoon. He watched the butterfly for a long time. Feeling sorry for it, he decided to help it out. He took a razor blade and gently slit open its cocoon to help the butterfly emerge. However, a few days later he noticed that the butterfly was still there. It never flew. He wondered, "What happened? Did I do something wrong?" Then it occurred to him that he had given the butterfly too much help. In doing so, he had deprived the butterfly of the struggle it needed to develop its own strength to get out of the cocoon by itself.

People are similar. If they are helped too much, it weakens them. Like the butterfly, they can be deprived of the struggle necessary for them to develop sufficient strength of character on their own.

For example, parents who have been doing for their children what their children can do for themselves have been depriving them of the struggle they need to develop on their own. Parents who have not been giving their children household chores to do have been failing them. Likewise, parents who have not been properly disciplining their kids have been failing them.

Do you love your child?

If so, then have him or her do age-appropriate chores, like taking out the garbage, straightening up the room, making the bed, cutting the grass, raking the leaves, shoveling snow. Have him or her clear the table and help with the dishes. When she is old enough, teach her how to cook, wash clothes, and iron.

On the other hand, if you were to do it all for your children, you would be helping them out of their "cocoons" too soon. They would become lazy, impatient, lack persistence and become overly dependent upon you and others. In short, they would become literally "spoiled," weakened in character and not adequately prepared for life. Conversely, when you assign your child responsibilities he or she will become responsible and have more character, just as *not* giving the child responsibilities will cause the child to become irresponsible and have less character, a dangerous state to be in.

Think of people you know or know of and observe the truth of this axiom. When people share in responsibilities, work, and so forth, they simply become better, stronger people: people with character.

What I have just described is the same reason welfare does not work. Welfare reduces people to a state of dependency because they have been "helped" too much by the government. Consequently, we find third, fourth, and even fifth generations in this country trapped in welfare, as evidenced by widespread Section-8 housing and the ubiquitous housing "projects" in cities across the land, with their high crime rates, substance abuse, absent fathers, births out of wedlock, chronic unemployment, and poverty.

Character weaknesses spawn all kinds of social ills, including suicide.

Government will not solve the problem. Instead, government is a large part of the problem and perpetuates the situation. Consider failed government projects everywhere, especially in our inner cities. The reason socialism never works, and never will work, is because it "helps" people too much. Abraham Lincoln once said "that government should only do for its people what the people cannot and/or will not do for themselves" – such as building roads and armies. People will not build roads and they will not build armies. Almost everything else should be privatized, including education, where government has also failed, miserably. With regards to what people can and will do for themselves, government should get out of the way, and let people do for themselves. When people do things for themselves they do it much better, and they become independent while becoming stronger in character.

It is *vital* that people be stronger in character because character weaknesses are debilitating and often ruin lives and can on occasion lead to death, as I will show. After God, it is safe to say that character may be the most important element in our lives. If fact, later in this text we will see that the Bible provides many scriptures about character.

Study Guide —Chapter 1

Try coming up with the answers on your own, as a mental exercise, before looking them up:

1. What is the moral of the anecdote of the butterfly? Pg. 5.

2. How are people similar to the butterfly? Pg. 5.

3. What causes people to become strong and independent? Pgs. 5–8.

4. What causes people to become weak and dependent? Pgs. 5–8.

Chapter 2

What is character?

First of all, this chapter too is a description of character, not a definition, and it is my opinion only. The reason I state this is my opinion only is because I do not claim to be an expert on character. But then again, are there any experts on the subject of character? I have never heard of one, and that fact is ironic for such an important matter. When I started writing this book, I had never seen a book or an article written about this elusive subject of character, and defining it. Nor am I aware of any college courses or studies on character. On rare occasions, I have heard of courses concerned with some of the character traits only. Yet the more I look into the topic, the more I notice that character is a vast and important subject. This writing is perhaps a trail blazing attempt to uncover the nature of what character is specifically, because character is so vital to our success and well being. It is a basis upon which we elect people to public office, hire employees, choose who we want to do business with, choose our mates, friends, and so on. (Martin Luther King put an emphasis on character when, in his famous 1963 address, he said that he hoped his children "will not be judged by the color of their skin but by the content of their character").

There are at least forty character traits that I can determine, possibly more than fifty. A person with character has many, although not necessarily all, of the following character traits:

Self-control, self-discipline—exercises restraint when necessary. The Apostle Paul said, *I keep under my body, and bring it into subjection. (1 Corinthians 9:27).* Paul was self-disciplined and had tremendous self-control. He engaged in the grueling work, sacrifices, and sufferings necessary to spread the gospel throughout the known world in his time.

When you can control yourself you can accomplish anything with God's help.

Persistence, tenacity, stamina—doesn't give up when it is something he believes in.

Patience—knows when something is worth waiting for, working for, fighting for.

Hard working, has a good work ethic, diligent—is useful, productive, and fruitful. Doesn't seek handouts, something for nothing, get-rich-quick schemes. Does not cheat or gamble. Not afraid of hard work or getting hands dirty. Is not lazy and often goes the extra mile. Has stamina. Works for what he gets. Does not rest on laurels and past accomplishments but keeps on going.

Is resilient—when he is knocked down, he doesn't stay there. He gets up again. When he fails, he tries again, and again if necessary. He does not easily give up. He is not easily defeated, discouraged or intimidated. He keeps on keeping on, with the attitude of either win or lose but not giving up. And he ends up winning all of the time or almost all of the time.

Is active—usually doing something.

Reliable, dependable—is punctual, does what is expected of him. Does what he says he will do. Is a man of his word.

Independent, self-reliant—is rugged, resourceful, and innovative. Makes do with what he has. Makes a little go a long way.

Dedicated, committed, determined, is purposed—is passionate, has strong will power, is steadfast in the face of opposition, has the courage of his or her convictions, does what's right whether popular or not, convenient or not, expedient or not.

Honest, trustworthy, ethical—someone you can rely on.

Moral—avoids temptations when he can, resists temptations.

Sincere, straightforward, forthright, frank, fair/just/impartial—A person of character means what he says and says what he means.

Principled—A person without principles is lacking in character. For example, many politicians are unprincipled. They just go with the flow of public sentiment, right or wrong. They have no courage or convictions. They simply want to have power, status, and wealth, be elected, and to be reelected. What is good for their constituencies takes a back seat to what is good for their political careers. There are two kinds of elected officials—statesmen and politicians. We have far too many politicians and too few statesmen. Statesmen are in the minority, although they have great character.

Patriotic, law abiding—a person with character is a good citizen and respects authority.

Obedient to God's Word—if a Christian.

Loves, caring, loyal, committed, protective—of family, loved ones, friends and others; is kind, compassionate, sympathetic, empathizing, supportive, encouraging, understanding, considerate, sensitive to the feelings and needs of others. Someone with character likes people, is friendly, respectful, does not envy. Read all of 1st Corinthians 13, which has been called the greatest description of love ever. (If the word "charity" appears in your translation, replace it with "love").

Hospitable, friendly—treats others as he or she would like to be treated. *Use hospitality one to another. (1 Peter 4:9).*

Generous, selfless—helps people, is almost always there when needed, prays for people, is altruistic, noble. Often puts others before himself or herself. "Will give you the shirt off of his back." *Give, and it shall be given unto you. (Luke 6:38).*

Is kind—doesn't try to hurt anyone, doesn't gossip, spread rumors, "backstab," "badmouth," or belittle people. Gives credit where credit is due. Is gracious to people.

Non-judgmental—sees the good in people, not a fault-finder, gives people the benefit of the doubt, doesn't have a critical spirit.

Forgiving, merciful—doesn't hold grudges or get "personal" with others; is magnanimous.

Not easily offended—is un-offendable, unflappable.

Humble—is teachable, has his ego under control, willing to serve.

Accepts constructive criticism—accepts correction, not offended by disagreements.

Admits he is wrong when he is—acknowledges or apologizes if he is at fault.

Modest—doesn't brag, does not try to impress, and is transparent.

Usually has a sense of humor—doesn't take himself too seriously.

Has a good attitude, thankful, generally positive—optimistic, "the glass is half full" type; not "the glass is half empty" type, not a complainer.

Has good habits—such as spending time regularly with God, family and friends; stays physically fit through physical activity, proper diet, and so on.

Is good, righteous, down to earth—wholesome, clean-cut, decent.

Has common sense—is realistic, practical, objective, and has perspective.

Responsible, conscientious—is decisive, assertive.

Has initiative—a self-starter, self-motivated, proactive, does things now rather than procrastinating; has a "get-up-and-go" nature.

Organized—is methodical, plans, sets goals.

Thinks ahead, has foresight, prepares for the future—exercises self-sacrifice and self-denial for long-term gain; puts needs ahead of wants, sees the big picture, sees the woods and the trees.

Thrifty, saves, prudent, a good steward—of money, resources and time.

Brave, courageous—generally fearless, bold, not overly cautious in taking risks.

Confident (without arrogance)—self-assured and comfortable with himself or herself; good self-image, secure.

Has dignity—self-respect.

Balanced—moderate, temperate, doesn't engage in excesses.

After reading the above list, by now you may feel a little overwhelmed. However, don't fret; there may be no one alive who has all of these traits, since none of us are perfect. Instead, all of us have strengths and weaknesses. If you recognize some of your weaknesses, reading further will show how you can strengthen them.

As you can see, many of the character traits overlap each other; and the subject of character is very broad and in-depth, simply because it is comprised of such an abundance of traits. The traits could also be called the "attributes," "pillars," or "functions" of character. It really doesn't matter what they are called. I prefer to call them "traits" for simplicity. Perhaps you can think of more character traits.

Most people have character to varying degrees. Anyone with a majority of these traits has strong character, and is often referred to as a person "of character" or a person with "substance" or "depth." Few people, if any, have all of these traits. Likewise, few people have none of them. Most of us fall somewhere in between. If you are missing only a few of these traits, you still have great character, but you have a character weakness in one or more areas, and most of us, if not all of us, have some character weaknesses somewhere. These can be strengthened.

Some of my own character weaknesses have been things like lateness and procrastination.

Study Guide —Chapter 2

Try coming up with the answers on your own, as a mental exercise, before looking them up:

1. Name and describe at least six character traits. Pgs. 10–14.

2. Which trait is most important to you, and why?

3. Can you think of any other character trait(s) not listed in this chapter?

4. Are you aware of any character traits you feel you need strengthening in your life? *(Remember, practically all of us have some character strengths and weaknesses to varying degrees.)*

Chapter 3

How Do We Get Character?

Just as muscles are developed (for example, from lifting weights, hard physical labor, sports) character is likewise developed—knowingly or unknowingly—from struggle, work, adversity, responsibilities, activity, hardships, discipline, training, doing without, problem solving, etc. To continue still further, character comes through learning from failures, mistakes, setbacks, disappointments, and from life experiences. In short, character comes from years of work and an active life—"from the school of hard knocks." Character can also be instilled, grounded, and inculcated into young people by good parents, churches, teachers, mentors, good friends, and good role models. As you can see, character comes from a variety of sources.

Character doesn't come quickly or easily. You will find that anyone who has great character has not had an easy life, particularly during his or her formative years. It cannot come in any other way. You "pay your dues" for character. Once you have it, character is *priceless*. It enables us to reach our full potential and to bless and benefit our loved ones, others, and our world. Character enables us to lead prosperous, abundant, and full lives and helps us to benefit and provide for others.

So God permits us to go through these hardships, trials and tribulations, which is why some people question, "If there is a God, then why are there so many problems in the world?" One reason God permits problems to exist in the world is to develop us. Does His Word support this claim that struggling with problems and situations strengthens our character? Yes. The Word says, *We glory in tribulations also: knowing that tribulation worketh patience; And patience, experience; and experience, hope. (Romans 5:3-4).* This is about character, isn't it? Yet, evidentially the word "character" did not exist in Biblical times, because the word "character" does not appear anywhere in scripture. However, many scriptures refer to character traits.

A great Biblical example of how tribulation and struggle develop strength of character is in the Book of Exodus. Thousands of years ago, in the land of Canaan (now modern day Israel), there was virtually no food in the land. To avoid starvation, Joseph's family moved from the land of Canaan to Egypt where it was known there was plenty of food. Over the next 400 years, the Jews multiplied and became very numerous, to the extent that the King of Egypt became alarmed. *And he said unto his people, Behold, the people of Israel are more and mightier than we; Come on, let us deal wisely with them; lest they multiply, and it come to pass, that, when there falleth out any war, they join also unto our enemies, and fight against us, and so get them up out of the land. Therefore they did set over them taskmasters to afflict them with their burdens. And they built for Pharaoh treasure cities, Pithom and Raamses.* ***But the more they afflicted them, the more they multiplied and grew.****" (Exodus 1:9-12).*

Notice that highlighted sentence above. You would think that the more the Egyptians oppressed the Jewish people, the weaker and fewer in number they would have become. Instead, the exact opposite happened. The Jewish people became stronger and multiplied, through the "exercise" of the hardships. God, in his "tough love," was preparing the Israelis to become strong enough to leave Egypt on their own, to return to their own promised land of Canaan, which they eventually did. When they finally left Egypt none of them were weak.—*there was not one feeble person among their tribes. (Psalm 105:37).* Can you imagine that?! Out of several million people, not one of them was sick or weak. They had become strong in body and in character. Although they did not recognize it at the time, God had made them strong by allowing them to go through their ordeals. *The refining pot is for silver, and the furnace for gold: but the Lord trieth the hearts. (Proverbs 17:3).* Yes, God knows what He is doing; although we do not always know what He is doing, and why He is doing it. And we often question Him. *For who hath known the mind of the*

Lord? (Romans 11:34). For thou, O God, hast proved us: thou hast tried us, as silver is tried. Thou hast brought us into the net' thou laidst affliction upon our loins... we went through fire and through water: but thou broughtest us out into a wealthy place. (Psalms 66:10-12).

Similarly, after the crucifixion of Christ, persecution soon broke out against the Christians. Many of them were arrested, tortured, and killed. But nothing could stop them. Christians became more determined than ever to spread the good news of the Gospel to the then-known world; and look at what we have today.

In the early church, the martyr, St. Justin Martyr, who lived in the second century stated, "We are slain with the sword, but we increase and multiply; the more we are persecuted and destroyed, the more are deaf to our numbers. As a vine, by being pruned and cut close, shoots forth new suckers, and bears a greater abundance of fruit; so it is with us."[1]

Today in China, since 1949 there has been relentless persecution of Christians. Similar to 2,000 years ago, Christians in China today are hunted down, arrested, beaten, and some of them tortured and killed on a regular basis. *Because* of the persecutions and hardships borne by Christians in

---

[1]Used by Permission *The Voice of the Martyrs*, www.persecution.com, PO Box 443, Bartlesville, OK 74005, 1-918-337-8015, www.persecution.com, thevoice@vom-usa.org.

China today, they are spreading the Gospel throughout the country. According to the Nora Lam Chinese Ministries International, over 25,000 Chinese become Christians every *day*.

So, whenever the going gets rough and problems arise, don't get mad at God. He loves you and is allowing things to happen to strengthen you for the plans He has for you. Or He may be trying to get your attention for some other reason. But how you react to it is what counts. You can keep on struggling or give up. Keep at it and work and wait while God does His work on you, and see what happens. Remember, *they that wait upon the Lord shall renew their strength; they shall mount up with wings as eagles; they shall run, and not be weary; and they shall walk, and not faint. (Isaiah 40:31).* Joseph struggled and waited, and look what happened. Job struggled and waited, and look what happened. Just keep on struggling and trust God no matter what life throws your way. Go by *faith, and not by sight. (2 Corinthians 5:7).*

You can deduce that anyone with great character was not raised in luxury, or "with a silver spoon in his mouth," or "spoiled" and pampered. I don't know of any that have. Do you? These "spoiled" people suffer from what is called "arrested development," due to the lack of sufficient struggle and work. Consequently, these are the people who want bigger and bigger government to take care of them because they have difficulty in taking care of themselves. However, "arrested development" [of character] can be reversed, which will be explained later in this writing.

It is a fact that many truly successful people have come from relatively poor, yet hard, working-class, families. They have often had to struggle and make do with what they had, or had to do without. Little or nothing was handed to them. They've worked for everything they had. All of their struggles, problems and over comings were stimulating; and it is stimulation that produces growth in character, as well as growth in everything else.

As the saying goes, "He's raised himself by his own boot straps" or is a "self-made man." (Of course, it's God who orchestrates it all). But the successful person often started working at an early age, perhaps delivering newspapers, cutting grass, opening up a lemonade stand. (Any kind of honest work develops character.) And if he had smart parents, he was given chores and responsibilities to do around the house. By having responsibilities, he has become responsible. His parents have not been doing many things for him that he could do for himself. So he has developed character, along with good work habits and good habits in general. This is how character is developed. It cannot come in any other way. Nobody is born with character. But we are all born with the potential of strong character.

Many people of strong character have been raised on farms or in the country where there are not a lot of conveniences, so they've had to work hard, persist, and make do with what they had. Many others have been in sports that require work, effort, practice, practice, practice, self-discipline, and sweat. Many have had good educations, which, likewise, require work, study, practice, self-discipline, persistence, and patience.

Character can be imparted into children by the example set for them by hardworking parents. Many have received proper discipline and structure from parents, from schools, or from the military. Again, through years of work, struggle, and activity, character is developed. Examples of such people are Abraham Lincoln, Thomas Edison, Andrew Carnegie, Dr. Ben Carson, and successful people from all walks of life. You can think of some. You may be one of them or on your way to becoming one of them.

Smart parents administer loving discipline to their children. If a child misbehaves, he is made to pay the consequences by being spanked (but not beaten, of course). Although some states prohibit corporal punishment, which is unfortunate. *He that spareth his rod hateth his son: but he that loveth him chasteneth him. (Proverbs 13:24). Chasten thy son while there is hope, and let not thy soul spare for his crying. (Proverbs 19:18). Foolishness is bound in the heart of a child; but the rod of correction shall drive it far from him. (Proverbs 22:15). Withhold not correction from the child: for if thou beatest him with the rod, he shall not die. Thou shalt beat him with the rod, and shalt deliver his soul from hell. (Proverbs 23:13-14).* Or the child is reprimanded, made to stand in the corner for a while, is "grounded," or has something taken away from him. In short, a child *has* to be taught. If left to his own devices, a child would, in essence, be "raising" himself. He would become a problem and give grief to his parents. *The rod and reproof give wisdom: but a child left to himself bringeth his mother to shame. (Proverbs 29:15). Correct thy son, and he shall give thee rest; yea, he shall give delight unto thy soul. (Proverbs. 29:17).* So structure, discipline, and the enforcing the limits instill character in a child—character that pays rich dividends later in life. He feels more secure by knowing what the limits are and that someone is in charge. He learns right from wrong, is better balanced, better adjusted, and better prepared for life. He also develops more respect for his parents, and he may well thank them later in life. Discipline is Biblical. *Thou shalt also consider in thine heart, that as a man chasteneth his son, so the Lord thy God chasteneth thee (Deuteronomy 8:5).*

Do you love your children? Be an example for them. If you work hard, the chances are they will work hard. If you are honest the chances are that they will be honest. If you don't smoke, the chances are that they will not smoke. The same can be said for the other character traits. Children copy what you do much more than what you say. When you are a good role model for your kids you, greatly increase their chances of success as they develop and mature. They will be a wonderful blessing to you and to others. To boot, you will reduce or completely eliminate the chances of your children ever becoming a criminals, addicts, or homeless. Love your family? Strengthen your character!

Strong character is as essential for a good life just as water is essential to life. For example, no one can become successful without being persistent. Another example: no one can become successful without being patient. No one can be successful without self-control. Without self-control one would be prone to addictions, bad habits, and laziness. As an exercise, you can take the other character traits and can come up with similar examples. Yes, strong character is essential for a full, useful, and prosperous life.

Study Guide —Chapter 3

Try coming up with the answers on your own, as a mental exercise, before looking them up:

1. Where does character come from? How do we get it? Pgs. 17–25.
2. How did the Egyptian oppressions against the people of Israel eventually enable the Jewish people to leave Egypt? Pgs. 18–20.
3. How did persecution of the early church result in the spreading of the Gospel, and, even today, the spreading of the church in countries like China? Pgs. 20 & 21.

Chapter 4

How Can We Strengthen Our Character?

If you should find yourself to be weak in character in some ways, "be of good cheer." We all have strengths and weaknesses. *No* one is without hope. You can strengthen your character yourself, although it won't be easy or quick. Nevertheless you can do it! You have to. You have no other choice but to strengthen your character if you want to live the full, fruitful, abundant life God has planned for you, and to make a difference in the lives of others.

As to how to strengthen our character, I would like to start with an example. Say that we want to build up muscle. We do so by exercising, lifting weights, working out, etc. Similarly, when you want to build up your character, do a "character workout"—namely by doing things you *should* do, even if you don't feel like doing them. Some things that we should do will be difficult or just a plain hassle. But, when we do them anyway, we grow a little stronger in our character each time we do them—even if we don't notice our growth.

Do yourself a favor. Strengthen your character! It will save you grief, and perhaps the grief of others. You will reap rewards over time, some of them being:

- It will help to keep you out of trouble.
- It will help preserve your marriage, family, and other relationships.
- It will help you keep your livelihood.
- You will be healthier, fit, and look better.
- It will keep you off of addictions.
- It may save you from depression and other health issues.
- It may keep you out of jail, avert suicide, or otherwise save your life.
- It will make your family blessed and stronger by your example and your provision.
- It will improve your self-image. You will feel better about yourself.
- Others will benefit because of you because you will make a difference in their lives.
- It will greatly increase your chances of success.
- Last, but not least, and *most* important, it will increase your chances of going to heaven.

You can't go wrong by observing the right do's and don'ts. The best book on do's and don'ts is the Bible—the only book ever written by God. Take advantage of it. You cannot go wrong with just doing what the Bible says. Bill Britt, a successful businessman from Chapel Hill, North Carolina, once said, "The Bible works, even if you don't believe in God." But when you read it (preferably aloud) your faith and belief will also steadily increase.

The *harder* it is to do what we *should* do, the more the act of doing it adds to our character. It might be:

- working
- fixing something
- studying
- practicing
- helping someone
- facing a fear by doing what you are afraid to do
- asserting yourself
- learning something new (which also retards the aging process, by the way)
- getting up and going to work
- sexual abstinence outside of marriage
- turning down a cigarette, or a drink, or a "fix," or any harmful temptation like overeating, over spending, gambling
- giving

- sharing
- practicing hospitality
- being honest, frank, forthright
- avoiding trying to impress others

The following are examples of how we can strengthen our character.

DEPENDENCY: Do you find yourself being overly dependent upon others to doing things for you, to provide for you, or make decisions for you? You can overcome that dependency that would otherwise continue to making you weaker, by becoming independent and self-reliant. Simply do more things for yourself that you can do, instead of letting someone else do them for you. Simple enough? In time you will find yourself becoming stronger. Over dependency is a character weakness, which you want to avoid. Make it a habit. Start out small if you have to, and build up from there. Don't worry about making mistakes. You will make some mistakes and have experiences and learn from them. It's called a "learning curve." By doing more things for yourself you will be "exercising" the independent, self-reliant traits in your character.

PROCRASTINATION: Do you have the tendency to procrastinate to avoid doing a job or project? Perhaps you find that things are piling up on you and you are way behind on things needing to be done around the house, your yard, your car, your job, business, or whatever needs being done. To remedy that situation, start out by doing just one thing a day, like fixing something, cleaning something, eliminating clutter, making a call. By doing just one thing a day you will be surprised how much you will get done over time. Of course, this involves a measure of self-discipline, which helps us to break the procrastination habit—a common character "ailment." Getting just one thing done can often motivate us to do still one or more things. By completing one task a day (which won't "kill" you) without missing a day, you will be surprised how much you accomplish and you'll finish sooner than you expected. (Dr. Robert Schuller once said, "Inch by inch everything's a cinch; yard by yard everything's hard.")

Sometimes, when I am working on two or three projects simultaneously, like taxes, carpentry, and writing, I'll do at least one thing a day on each of them and find myself completing all of them eventually, and often sooner than expected. And if I can do it, you can do it, because as I mentioned earlier, procrastination has been one of my character shortcomings.

LATENESS: Are you are prone to being late? If so, practice being early once a day for something like being to work on time, attending a birthday party, paying a bill. Unfortunately, I've found that simply trying to be on time doesn't always work; for I am still often a few minutes late anyway. So I tried something else. Instead of just trying to be *on time*, I tried being *early*. It worked, even though I would arrive there seconds earlier. Exactly why, I don't know. But it works for me.

TELEVISION-WATCHING: I believe that literally millions of people are addicted to television (an unrecognized and undiagnosed epidemic). Do you think that you might be one of them? If, by chance, you are a "couch potato" and want to get rid of that addiction, start by abstaining from watching television for one or two hours a day, or one day a week—whatever you think you can stand. You will find that as you watch a little less, you'll live a little more; and you will be surprised how much more you will get done, such as taking more time with your family, friends, or finishing work.

There is no doubt in my mind that excessive television watching slowly weakens our character through inactivity. That is what "vegetating" in front of the television means. We have all heard the expression, "If you don't use it you lose it." Well, when we are watching television we're using nothing, except our fingers on the remote. So, excessive television watching entertains us while it weakens us. Our bodies weaken. Our muscles atrophy. We become flabby physically, mentally, and emotionally. So, excessive television watching not only weakens our character, it also weakens us mentally and physically because no work or effort, manual dexterity, activity, intellect or imagination or mental exercise of any kind is involved. All we have to do is sit there and watch and do nothing.

I might add that our relationships also slowly deteriorate, because we spend too much time "relating" with the television rather than with family and people.

Many parents also use the television as a "babysitter." This is a mistake. Television likewise gives us the "escape" to avoid doing things that need to be done, like fixing something, cleaning something, and cutting the grass. Excessive television spawns a host of problems. Get away from it. Do I have a television? Yes. But it collects dust. In the past four years, as I remember, I've watched two presidential State of the Union Addresses, and a three or four videos and DVD's.

Abstaining from television gradually adds to our strength of character. Abstaining from television helps strengthen our marriages, and our other relationships. Abstaining from television helps us to get more things done. In fact, in addition to abstaining from television or any other harmful addictions such as smoking, drinking, drugs, porn, sex outside of marriage and sin, further "exercises" our character, strengthening it.

We will return to this topic of television below.

OVERWEIGHT: Are you overweight because of overeating or laziness? If so, then once a day cut down on carbohydrates or sweets or portion sizes. Or walk twenty minutes a day, or do some other physical activity. Again, *anything* that you do for twenty-one consecutive days becomes a habit.

However, if you have any health issues, you should check with your doctor first before embarking on a weight reduction program. Losing weight is a character builder because each time you do something to lose weight you will strengthen the self-discipline aspects of your character.

IMPULSE BUYING: Are you an impulse buyer, a "spendaholic," or materialistic? To help solve that problem, when you see something you want, just wait a day. By the next day you will find that your craving for it has diminished or disappeared. *There is treasure to be desired and oil in the dwelling of the wise; but a foolish man spendeth it up. (Proverbs 21:20).* So if you don't want to slowly go broke, when you see something you want to buy, just ask yourself if you *need* it or just *want* it. The problem is that many people don't consider the difference between needs and wants. When you consider needs versus wants, you will cut down your over-spending and debt, and you will be a better steward of what God has given you. It will also help you to avoid unwanted clutter in your home. Clutter presents its own problems such as less organization, less living space, making it harder to find things, some added stress, possible tripping, and mildew. Exercising restraint in spending and accumulating things also strengthens the self-denial trait in our character.

LITTLE OR NO SAVINGS: If you are in the habit of not saving money, then just save at least, for example, a dollar a day for twenty-one days. Or save on a weekly basis for twenty-one consecutive weeks—whatever is doable for you. When you do something for twenty-one consecutive days or times, it no longer remains a hassle. But if you miss a day, start over again until it becomes a habit. Moreover, saving adds to the self-discipline aspect of our character.

Excessive borrowing: If you're a "borrowaholic," using credit for practically everything you buy, try paying for something in cash at least once a day, or once a week. Do this for twenty-one consecutive days or times until it becomes a habit. Like savings, paying for things with cash will help get you slowly get out of debt and stay out of debt, and costing you less, in the long run, for whatever you buy. Millions of people are unknowingly "borrowaholics" (another unrecognized epidemic) and most of these people are in financial trouble, which gives rise to a host of other problems, such as marital, stress, and health, to name a few.

The word "credit" sounds good, but the more credit we have, the more ability we have to go into more debt. Nevertheless, with credit, the temptation is always there to use it excessively.

Credit also gives us a false sense of security because it makes us think we have more than we do. Because of this, we can easily spend more that we can afford and get into hopeless debt. The Bible cautions us against borrowing. *Owe no man any thing. (Romans 13:8)* and *the borrower is servant to the lender. (Proverbs 22:7).*

If you have credit cards, pay them off at the end of the month if you are able to, to avoid the interest charges, and to help you to be more accountable to your "checkbook." If you are unable to pay off the balance on your credit card then pay more than the amount due monthly until you are paid off.

Don't carry around a lot of money with you so as to avoid the temptations of buying things you don't need. Likewise, you might not want to carry credit cards with you either, for the same reason and if you don't think you will need them on any particular day. Carry just a little more than you think you will need. Paying for things in cash, when you are able to, likewise strengthens our self-control as well as the prudent aspect of our character.

SELF-CENTEREDNESS: Are you self-centered or selfish? If so, it is a good bet you are not enjoying life very much. Am I right? You're probably lonely, lack real friends, joy, peace, security, fulfillment, and blessings. For example, if you occasionally have a need, you are probably too embarrassed to ask a neighbor for help because you have no relationships with any of your neighbors. You may even resort to your television for "company." Many examples can be given. Again, please understand I am not judging anyone, because we *all* have strengths and weaknesses. I used to be somewhat self-centered myself, and looking back in retrospect, it didn't do me any good. So I am also "preaching" to myself here.

To help remedy your situation, there are a number of steps you can take:

1. Call someone just to say "Hello" or to ask how they are doing.
2. Visit someone; invite someone to church.
3. Do someone a favor.
4. Help someone.
5. Volunteer for something.

Give of your time or of yourself until it becomes a lifestyle. We get back what we give, often multiplied. It's the so-called "Law of Reciprocity." *Give, and it shall be given unto you. For with the same measure that ye mete withal it shall be measured to you again. (Luke 6:38).* The Bible has much to say about giving and the benefits of giving.

Giving is also self-fulfilling. For example, have you ever noticed that when you gave a present to someone who needed it, that when they opened the present you were as excited as they were!? Or when you helped someone in need you were blessed too, as though it happened to you? *It is more blessed to give than to receive. (Acts 20:35).*

Therefore, be a giver and not a taker. Rather than being self-centered, be God–centered and other-people-centered. *Thou shalt love the Lord thy God with all thy heart, and with all thy soul, and with all thy mind. (Matthew 22:37)* and *Thou shalt love thy neighbor as thyself. (Matthew 22:39).* It pays bigger rewards. Focus on what God wants, as well as the needs and wants of others, and you'll find something to talk about or do. Be friendly. To have a friend is to be a friend. *A man that hath friends must show himself friendly. (Proverbs 18:24).* Invite someone over. *Be a lover of hospitality. (Titus 1:8).* Give of yourself. Give of your love. *Love never fails.* (*Corinthians 13:8*).

I know a woman who is a taker and not a giver, and she is a chronic complainer. She is in constant need—often asking for help and favors—and has financial, health and other problems. She almost never has any visitors, including from family. It is very sad and pitiful. If she had been a giver, she would have had a much better and fulfilling life.

When we give, God abundantly rewards us, sooner or later, in one way or another. It could be said that "giving is enlightened selfishness." Thus if you are self-centered and lonely, become a giver. Give of your love. Give of your time, your money, your substance, if necessary give of yourself. And it will come back to you. Giving also adds to and strengthens the trait of generosity of our character.

INSECURITY: Are you fearful, timid, shy, introverted, uncomfortable being around people, or insecure in general? To help fix that situation, occasionally say or do something you normally would not have said or done, whether it is speaking your mind, standing your ground, asserting yourself, exercising authority, or speaking in public. I know it's easier said than done. But it is a great exercise, and you can do it. There's no other way, if you ever want to come out of your shell. Do it quickly; otherwise, if you think about it too much, the chances are you may never do it.

You must face your fears, because the Word says, *The fear of man bringeth a snare: but whoso putteth his trust in the Lord shall be safe. (Proverbs 29:25).* God wants us to trust Him. He's here to help you. However, unbelief is a sin. So get over your fears. You can do it. Remember, you *can do all things through Christ* who strengthens you. *(Philippians 4:13).* And, His *strength is made perfect in weakness. (2 Corinthians 12:9).* Mark Twain said, "Do the thing you fear most and the death of fear is certain." Face your fears. When you make yourself do something that normally you've been afraid to do, your fears *will* slowly but surely subside—probably every time you do it—thereby "exercising" the bravery and courage traits of your character.

Short-temperedness: If you are short-tempered, you might try biting your tongue or at least "counting to ten" when situations arise that "bug" you. You have to practice controlling your tongue, because when you stop to think about it, you may have noticed the unbridled tongue has helped cause broken relationships, unforgiveness, job losses, divorces, and dysfunctional families. Often, the unbridled tongue has contributed to emotional scars, emotional illnesses, low self-images, wrong decisions, adverse changes of destiny, fights, killings, conflicts, wars. *He that is soon angry dealeth foolishly (Proverbs 14:17).* On the other hand, *He that is slow to wrath is of great understanding (Proverbs 14:29).* And *He that is slow to anger is better than the mighty (Proverbs 16:32).*

Here is what the Bible has to say about the tongue in comparing it to the rudder of a ship. *Behold also the ships, which though they be so great, and are driven of fierce winds, yet are they turned about with a very small helm, whithersoever the governor listeth. Even so the tongue is a little member, and boasteth great things. Behold, how great a matter a little fire kindleth! (James 3:4-5). For he that will love life, and see good days, let him refrain his tongue from evil. (1 Peter 3:10).*

It is all right to get angry, as long as we don't get personal by attacking, belittling, condemning or hurting others. In other words, *Be ye angry, and sin not: let not the sun go down upon your wrath. (Ephesians 4:26).* That is, attack the problem, not the person. But, if you slip up and make a mistake, simply go to the person and apologize. When you control your tongue you further strengthen the self-control trait of your character.

Remember, God is not asking us to be "doormats". When you think you are right and come under attack, just stand your ground, but do so without getting personal about it.

On the other hand, if you are short-tempered too much, it is possible you are bi-polar, and may need an evaluation.

Negative thinking: Are you overly skeptical or cynical? Are you a chronic complainer? Do you have a critical spirit? In short, do you have a negative attitude? Negative thinking is nothing more than a habit. God is displeased with negative thinking, complaining, and the like. In *Numbers 14:26-29* God said to Moses and Aaron that he was going to kill everyone from twenty years old and upward for murmuring and complaining against Him. God does not like complaining. In fact, nobody likes it. You and I don't like it either. People tend to avoid negative people because they are a drain on those who are around them. Conversely, people tend to be drawn to positive people. Having a sense of humor doesn't hurt either. Have you noticed that mumbling and grumbling don't make you happy? Mumbling, grumbling, criticizing, and complaining do not make anybody happy. So why do it? Negative thinking is a habit, and like any habit, it can be broken.

So, how do we kick the negative thinking habit? When you have a negative or critical thought about someone or something, replace that thought with a positive one about that same person or situation. Practice seeing the good in people, things, situations, and life until it becomes a habit. Look on the other side—the positive side of things. Or "count your blessings," as the saying goes. You will find you have far more to be thankful for than to complain about.

For example, if you had been suffering from blindness for many years and then miraculously and suddenly received your eyesight again, you immediately start yelling and screaming words like, "I can see! I can see!! Thank God I can see!!! You would hop up and down, run around, and tell everyone what happened to you. You'd go crazy with excitement. Well, as it is right now, you and I can see, or I wouldn't be writing this and you wouldn't be reading this. So why aren't we just as excited that we can see too? It's a mystery to me. Human nature being what it is, we typically have to lose something in order to appreciate it. Most of us can see, hear, walk, *and* have the use of our faculties, any one of which is of *infinite* value to us. If we were to lose any *one* of these blessings, we would pay any price to have it back. Isn't that true? Yet most of us have all of them. Most of us also have a roof over our heads, food in the refrigerator, money in our pockets, running water, heat, light, air-conditioning, cars, family, friends, any one of which, if suddenly gone, we would miss and appreciate a whole lot more. Again, there is *much* to be thankful for that most of us have right under our noses and normally don't even think about, unless it is gone. We've been taking our blessings for granted. I include myself in this assessment.

Each of us would benefit by training ourselves to count our blessings. And I am speaking to myself as well as to anyone else, because I have to keep reminding myself what I have.

Other forms of negativity include gossiping and backstabbing. When I hear someone making disparaging remarks about someone else, I immediately begin to distrust that person because I wonder what he may say about me behind my back. Badmouthing someone makes the criticizer and the one he is criticizing both look bad, and usually the one doing the criticizing looks worse than the one being criticized. That's the reason for the saying, "If you can't say something good about someone, don't say anything." On the other hand, if you make a habit of not bad-mouthing people, people will naturally be more inclined to trust you. *Whisperers* [i.e. gossipers] and *backbiters... are worthy of death. Romans 1:29-32).* God doesn't like it either.

We need to get rid of negative thinking habits, because negative thinking brings negative results. Negative thinking has never given anyone an abundant or successful life. As a man *thinketh so is he. (Proverbs 23:7)* and *bringing into captivity every thought to the obedience of Christ. (2 Corinthians 10:5).* You can "capture" (i.e. counter) negative thoughts with the use of scriptures. For example, if you think you cannot do something, you can "capture" that thought with something like, *I can do all things through Christ which strengtheneth me. (Philippians 4:13).* Or if you are worried about paying your bills, you can replace that thought with, *My God shall supply all my need according to his riches in glory by Christ Jesus. (Philippians 4:19).* Or if you are anxious about being harmed in some way, you can negate that worry with, *No weapon that is formed against* me *shall prosper. (Isaiah 54:17),* and so on. There are many scriptures that can change bad thinking habits into good thinking habits, because there is power in the Word (Hebrews 4:12). However, we need to study the Bible regularly in order to know which scriptures can help us with whatever we might be going through. In this way, you can control your thoughts, and controlling your thoughts strengthens the self-control and self-discipline aspects of your character.

THE SOMETHING FOR NOTHING MINDSET: Do you often find yourself trying to get something for nothing? Many of us have done that to varying degrees. But doing so weakens our character a little, every time—win or lose—while wasting some of our time. It's better to work for what we get—an exercise in persistence and patience.

Gamblers are a good example. When they win they're "motivated" to gamble again, hoping that "history will repeat itself." And when they lose they're still "motivated" to gamble again, hoping to get back what they've lost. So either way—win or lose—they are "motivated" to gamble again and again, thereby being trapped within a vicious cycle of trying to get "history to repeat itself" *or* trying to get back what they've lost, continuously. If a gambler doesn't have enough strength of character to quit while he is ahead or have enough strength to quit while he is behind to cut his losses, this vicious cycle eventually makes him become a "gambleaholic" and broke. That is what happened to my grandfather. He inherited a fortune and died penniless, from gambling on horse races in New York. My father had to quit college to help support his father.

Even when a gambler wins, his character is weakened a little, because the winning came easy. He didn't have to work for it. Therefore, he doesn't appreciate it as much; and it doesn't last as long. As the saying goes, "Easy come, easy go." On the other hand, when he works for something, he appreciates it more, he takes better care of it, and makes it last. He'll be a better steward of what he has. Whenever we get something for nothing, be it from gambling, cheating, or stealing, we are weakened a little each time (with the exceptions of receiving gifts, awards, etc., which of course is fine).

For example, back in the 1950's there was a popular television show called the "$64,000 Question" (a lot of money at the time). It is my understanding that ten years later a study was conducted of contestants that had won, and found that none of them still had the $64,000 and were no better off ten years later than they were before they had won the money.

The point is "There ain't no free lunch." "There's no such thing as something for nothing." You are very much better off working for what you get. *If any would not work, neither should he eat. (2 Thessalonians. 3:10).* Working for what we get rids us of the character weakness of laziness. It also helps to keep us honest and diligent. God does not like laziness or dishonesty, which are among the worst character weaknesses.

SUBMITTING YOURSELF TO DISCIPLINE: To build up your character, you might want to consider joining the military or enrolling in a military school. It is generally easier to be disciplined by others than it is to discipline ourselves.

MARRIAGE PROBLEMS: If you are married, is your marriage in trouble? Or has your marriage failed, and you desire reconciliation? Marriage is a vast subject. So, I am going to do my best to avoid going too far off on a tangent away from the subject of character. Yet, making a marriage work does require strong character and therefore is relevant to this discussion. Making a marriage work is also a great exercise in the building up of our character.

***

Believe it or not, men and women are not equal, as is the common belief among many today. And, needless to say, men and women are not alike. Each has strengths and weaknesses that compliment the other, and each helps make each other whole. I like the differences. God knew what He was doing when he made men men and women women.

God said, *Husbands, love your wives, even as Christ also loved the church. (Ephesians 5:25).* And, *Wives, submit yourselves unto your own husbands, as unto the Lord. For the husband is the head of the wife, even as Christ is the head of the church. (Ephesians 5:22- 23).* So wives submit to your husbands. A woman is more secure when she knows her husband is in charge and strong. So are the children.

Perhaps the biggest difference I've noticed between men and women is that, because men are the stronger sex and good providers, women naturally look up to men for protection, which is the way it should be. Women want security. Men want a challenge. So in a marriage there is nothing on earth more beautiful than one hand reaching down to protect and one hand reaching up for protection. It is part of God's design. I love it. I wouldn't have it any other way.

Because men are the stronger sex, it is the man's role to love, protect, and provide for his wife and his family. Likewise, it is his role to make the marriage work and to hold his family together. It is his role to exercise loving discipline and to set limits and structure in the family. It is his role to be an example to his family in the realm of commitment, loyalty, stability, breadwinning, being responsible, healthy living, maintenance of the home, yard, cars, anything that needs fixing. As Christ is head of the church, the man is head of his family. The wife's role is to submit to and support her husband, to cook, clean, "make the home a home," and take care of the kids. She really doesn't want a job outside of the home. She has a "full-time job" already taking care of the home. (However, I understand that high taxes force many mothers to work. When the government takes almost half of your income, you have to do something).

Because a woman is of the gentler, tender, fairer sex, it is the husband's role to cherish and protect her like a flower. He holds the door for her when she gets in the car. He never raises his voice at her. If they should have a spat, he later apologizes—whether he's right or wrong—or buys her a flower, or does something else to make up. A *man* certainly never tries to punish or hurt his wife mentally or physically. But *males* do. A *man* tries to meet her needs. But *males* may or may not. So don't be an insensitive jerk. Be aware of her needs. Be more than a *male*. Be a *man*. Men protect women and do not hurt them. Protect her and your family. Be tender with her, as you would be with a flower. I say this because today there are far too many single-parent families headed by women. Yes, we have plenty of males in America, but not enough men. (If you are a male, you can become a man by building up your character. I'm not trying to knock you down. I am trying to help build you up).

***

To strengthen or save your marriage, continue "courting" your wife. I say this because engaged couples get along well before they marry; but then after they marry, many men have essentially stopped doing what they did before marrying, namely courting their wives, which likewise can ultimately increase stress levels for the wives. The reason they stopped courting is because couples often tend to take each other for granted, a danger to any marriage. Don't fall into that trap. In other words, keep doing what you did before you got married, to keep your marriage. Why change what worked? When you were courting, you dated her. You took her out to dinner, to a movie, to the beach. You called her, bought her flowers, and more. Make courting a lifestyle. It is up to you men, and not up to her. It will simplify your life, is good for your kids, and is a whole lot better than going through the traumas and complications of a needless divorce. Because women are the weaker, fairer sex they need a break once in a while, preferably weekly. She needs an occasional change of scenery, a change of activity, a breather. She deserves it.

For example, once during my own marriage, for about four weeks my wife, Isabel, was in a bad mood. I didn't understand it. She would get mad about almost everything—even little things—and it made no sense to me. I would ask myself, "What's wrong with this girl?" I'd say or do something, and she would snap back something negative almost every time. She was jumpy. Something was bothering her.

Finally, one day God revealed to me what the problem was. Our two young sons and we had always eaten lunch together in a cafeteria after church on Sundays. But because of tight finances at that time, we had skipped eating in the cafeteria for four weeks, coinciding with Isabel's sour moods. God made me realize that, because of the lack of any breaks for Isabel from her busy schedule for four straight weeks, her stress level had increased. I quickly got the message. So, the next Sunday I made it a point to take the family back to the cafeteria again, and sure enough Isabel began to relax because there was nothing for her to do there except to eat and enjoy, and she began to lighten up and be her perky, colorful self again.

Since then, I have made sure we "dated" weekly thereafter, going to dinner, parties, visiting someone, walks, rides in the country, whatever came up. That solved the problem. It was an important lesson for me. So, if you and your wife are having some trouble in getting along, it could very well be that her stress level is up. Make sure she gets an occasional "breather," at least weekly. After all, she is your homemaker, the nanny if you have kids, cook, and among other things. She deserves it. Sometimes I would give Isabel other breaks by washing the dishes for her, vacuuming, and other chores to lighten her load and stress. Be creative. In fact, the more help, protection, and spending time with your wife the stronger your marriage will become—and the stronger you marriage the better your family life will become.

***

Men, be the decision maker. For example, if you are going out to a restaurant, you pick the restaurant that you think she would like. Your wife may suggest another restaurant, and another, but stick with your decision. She's probably subconsciously testing you. She wants you to make the decision. She wants to make sure she is married to a man. Nevertheless, consider her suggestions. But, after first talking with her, you make the decision, especially regarding major decisions. Communicate first.

***

Yes, a man is decisive, determined, dedicated and loyal. Therefore, he is committed to his marriage. Nevertheless, if you aren't committed to your marriage, I'm not judging you. You simply made some mistakes. And I hope I am addressing those mistakes for your benefit, and I hope you are getting something out of this. Commitment is vital to a marriage. When I first married, I decided that we would stay married no matter what—because both of us had seen enough divorces and separations. I had come from a broken family myself, and I'm familiar with the pain. So I told myself privately, "We're staying married." And there were times where we could have broken up, but we stuck it out. I have never regretted that decision. Persistence pays. When a man is committed to his marriage, he is in essence protecting his wife; and she knows it. She feels more secure and so do the kids. They know they have a family. You don't even have to say anything. They just know it. So one of the best things you can do for your kids is to love their mother. If you are divorced, I encourage you to at least forgive her or ask her to forgive you—no matter who's right or wrong—and attempt reconciliation. And, just start dating her again and see what happens. It worked the first time. It can work again.

***

Communication is vital to a marriage or any relationship. Make sure you spend enough time together. Talk to her. Tell her how pretty she is, and how your day has been, etc. Show her love, affection, and attention. Consider turning off the television, or just getting rid of it. Television is the biggest conversation robber there is, and a spoiler for marriages and family life, in general. It does much more harm than good. In fact, it doesn't do any good, with the exception of Christian programming. Google "television statistics" sometime and you will find eye-opening statistics of what television does to people. There is so much more we can *do* than just *watching* television anyway. We can play cards, games, sports, or talk with neighbors. At least, in doing so we're communicating. If you are not communicating much with your wife, then you are emotionally "divorced." You've become virtual "roommates." Save your marriage. Talk with her and your kids; they need your attention.

They need you. You need each other. That's the way God wants it. That is the way we are all "wired."

***

Pride can kill a marriage as quickly as anything, even without warning. Be careful of pride, particularly false pride. I have heard of couples splitting up over little things like arguing about which television program to watch. You are better off just knowing now that the two of you will sometimes have arguments and disagreements, but that is no reason to break up over. At least, when you are arguing you are communicating. You can always make up later. And you do not have to win every disagreement either. Someone once told me—with tongue-in-cheek - just two words can save a marriage, namely, "Yes dear!" I took that advice. So when I would have an argument with Isabel, and I saw that I wasn't getting anywhere, I'd jokingly say, "Yes dear!" And she would relax.

Unfortunately, sometimes a husband will stick his nose up in the air and say something like, "I'm going to teach her a lesson!" Or, "I'll never to talk to her again!" Or, "I'm leaving and never coming back!" That is false pride. That is being a *male*. It is also unforgiveness that will bring a curse such as sickness, an accident, or financial problems. God often chastises us to try and get our attention. *As many as I love, I rebuke and chasten. (Revelations 3:19)*. Pride and false pride are dangerous. Swallow your pride, go back to her, and make it right. Apologize. It takes a man to admit he is wrong, and to apologize. There is more than just your life that is affected. God blesses humility. He hates pride and even a proud look. *These six things doth the Lord hate...A proud look, a lying tongue, and hands that shed innocent blood. (Proverbs 6:16-17).* A Pastor once said, "Pride is the cause of all sin." As indicated above, humility is a character strength. False pride and arrogance are the opposite of humility and therefore character weaknesses, and nauseating as well. Get rid of them.

***

Addressing financial matters responsibly are important in a marriage. It has been said that "when poverty flies in the window, love flies out." So keep on top of your finances, one reason being that financial stress adds stress to the marriage. And it seems that most families today are facing financial stress—creating situations that can lead to our unacceptably high divorce rate. I encourage you to exercise restraint in spending and accumulating things. Wouldn't you rather have your marriage, family, and your money than a lot of things you don't need?

The very best and first step you can do to become financially solid is to tithe. *Will a man rob God? Yet ye have robbed me. But ye say, Wherein have we robbed thee? In tithes and offerings. Ye are cursed with a curse: for ye have robbed me... Bring ye all the tithes into the storehouse, that there may be meat in mine house, and prove me now herewith, saith the Lord of hosts, if I will not open you the windows of heaven, and pour you out a blessing, that there shall not be room enough to receive it. (Malachi 3:8-10).* This is the only place in the Bible where God says to *prove* Him, by tithing. And *Give, and it shall be given unto you... For with the same measure that ye mete withal it shall be measured to you again. (Luke 6:38).* In fact, I guarantee that when you tithe consistently, you will never be broke again. You may or may not get wealthy, but you will always have enough or more than enough. Do it! You can't go wrong by tithing.

***

A word for you wives. This may or may not be a big thing, depending on the strength of your marriage. I have known wives—that is Christian wives, married to Christian men—who were attractive when they first married, and after they got married they let themselves go. By overeating, lack of physical activity, and unhealthy living in general they became overweight, prematurely aged, and hence less attractive. Let's be honest, most husbands like to have attractive wives. So when wives let themselves go, *some* husbands begin to have "roving eyes," and sooner or later they are in the midst of an affair with another woman. One that I know left his wife and family of three daughters. Another got involved in pornography and tried hitting on other women, even in the church.

Therefore, I encourage you wives to stay fit and trim not only for health reasons, but for additional "insurance" for your marriage. Then again, your husband may well not cheat on you. But you don't want to take the chance, and you want to satisfy his needs anyway, which he deserves. In other words, wives, be smart. The less flab you have the more attractive you are. In fact, get and stay healthy, period. When you achieve health—by proper eating and by getting at least twenty or thirty minutes a day of some physical activity—your attractiveness will take care of itself. What you put in your mouth is infinitely more important than what you put on your face—as far as health and attractiveness are concerned.

By the way, have you noticed that anyone who is attractive is also healthy? So if you happen to have "let yourself go," get healthy again—a necessary ingredient to beauty, as well as a better life. I want the best for you. You can do it.

Finally wives, love your husband. Be affectionate, and submissive. Give him a reason to want to come home. Kids like it, too. Everybody does.

***

As you can see, a marriage warrants regular attention, in other words regular "maintenance," if you will. For example, when you buy a car, you know that periodically you have to change the oil, get it tuned up, get the front end aligned, and so fourth. You have to maintain your car or you will lose your car. Likewise, you have to maintain your marriage or you will lose your marriage or make it worse. And who wants that? Making a marriage work takes work. But it is work well worth doing. And it is not hard work anyway. The "work" required for a good marriage is far easier than the hardship and complications that result from a failed marriage. It is sad and a shame to see a marriage fail when simple things could have been done to prevent a breakup in the first place.

Obedience to the Word: I'm not trying to be "religious," but perhaps you have noticed that everything that strengthens character is Biblical. In fact, I have no doubt that the greatest character builder is simply doing what the Bible says. To put it another way, the less we sin, the more character we have, and the more we sin, the less character we have. So do yourself a favor: do what the Bible says as a lifestyle. It will change you and strengthen your character. It has changed me, and continues to change me, often without my being aware of it. It is not an overstatement to say that the Bible will help you have an impact upon the lives of your loved ones and of your world.

The problem is that most people have a Bible and ironically let it gather dust, a huge and tragic mistake. That costs them in this life and the in the eternity to come. *My people are destroyed* [in hell] *for lack of knowledge. (Hosea 4:6* says*).* So you do not want to lack Biblical knowledge, my friend—that is, the knowledge of what God wants and doesn't want. If God wrote me a letter, the first thing I would do is read it again and again. So would you. The Bible is God's love letter to you. He repeatedly pats you on the back and spanks you, because He loves you and wants to steer you in the right direction—to Him. Again, I urge you to read the Bible and do what it says. Simply doing what the Bible says is a great exercise in character building.

Every time you do something which requires effort that you should do—whether you feel like it or not—you strengthen your character, each time you do it.

Study Guide —Chapter 4

Try coming up with the answers on your own, as a mental exercise, before looking them up:

1. What is a "character workout?" Pg. 27.
2. What are some of the rewards of building up your character? Pg. 28.
3. What are some examples of doing things that add to your character? Pgs. 29 & 30.
4. How can you overcome over-dependency on others? Pg. 30.
5. How can you overcome the procrastination habit? Pgs. 30 & 31.

6. How can you overcome the habit of being late? Pgs. 31 & 32.

7. How many consecutive days does it take to make a habit? Pg. 35. What do you do if you break the habit? Pg. 35.

8. How can we break out of the excessive borrowing habit (and keep out of debt)? Pgs. 35 & 36.

9. What is the antidote to self-centeredness? Pgs. 36–38.

10. What are some of the remedies to insecurity, fearfulness, and timidity? Pgs. 38 & 39.

11. How can we control short-temperedness? Pgs. 39–41.

12. How can we break the negative thinking habit? Pgs. 41–44.

13. Regarding the "something for nothing" mindset, what should our attitude be? Pgs. 44–46.

14. Making a marriage work is a great exercise in ____________. Pg. 46.

15. In a marriage there is nothing more beautiful than one hand reaching down to ____________ and one hand reaching up for ____________. Pg. 47.

16. Regarding marriage, what should the husband's role be, and what should be the wife's role be? Pgs. 47 & 48.

17. What is meant by "courting your wife"? Why is it important? Pgs. 49 & 50.

18. Why should the man be the decision maker of major matters in a marriage? Pg. 51.

19. Why is television called a "conversation robber"? Pg. 52.

20. Why are pride and false pride dangerous to a marriage? Pgs. 53 & 54.

21. What is the best thing we can do to become financially sound? Pgs. 54 & 55.

22. If you don't maintain your marriage you may _______ your marriage. Pgs. 56 & 57.

23. Doing what the Bible says is a great exercise in ____________ building. Pg. 57.

Chapter 5
The Hazards of Weak Character

To get an idea of the critical importance of having strong character, consider the dangers of having weak character, from the following examples.

THE MATTER OF LACK OF SELF-CONTROL: Lack of self-control can result in your assaulting, raping, or killing someone. Or you could become involved with drugs, illicit sex, overspending, and other harmful things. If you had self-control you would not have these problems. Prisons are filled with people weak in character and weak in self-control. In fact, I believe it's safe to say that a population that has a high crime rate has what I will refer to as a low overall "character index," and a society with a low crime rate has a high overall "character index." Or, otherwise stated, the overall character index of a population is inversely proportional to its crime rate.

WITH REGARDS TO LACK OF PATIENCE: Lack of patience can result in your cheating, stealing, committing fraud and taking other "shortcuts" because you were not willing to wait and work for it, which of course can lead you to doing hard time in prison. Yes, weak character is dangerous.

For example, about thirty percent of the students in our public schools drop out, according to America's Promise Alliance, and more than fifty percent of the students in many of our largest cities drop out. This is due to character weaknesses such as lack of patience, lack of self-discipline, and lack of persistence. (To be fair, there are other contributing factors as well, such as poor public educational systems in the first place, dysfunctional families, fatherless families, escape mechanisms such as sex, drugs, alcohol, excessive television watching, excessive pleasure-seeking in general.)

So, in a large sense, we can't blame many of the kids from dropping out of school and thereby not nearly reaching their potential. Many of them also leave school out of sheer boredom because of the non-challenging "easy" curriculums that teach little if anything relevant in the public schools. Personally, I have no doubt there should be separation between government and education. It is clear that government has failed in public education. Yet, I am surprised there is so little public outcry about it. Government should get out of it. Even government officials and government politicians recognize that the government has failed in public education. They do not have their own children in public schools. Do they? Education should be privatized. Leave it up to us the people, not the government.

Many kids wonder "why stay in school." Then, when they drop out, they have a difficult time finding meaningful employment because they never learned how to do anything meaningful while in school (e.g. auto mechanics, plumbing, electronics, and other skills that mean something and are needed by prospective employers and society). So they end up in low-paying un-skilled jobs or turn to crime for a living or turn to drugs as an escape, in large part because of the lack of patience and persistence to finish school.

Wouldn't it be great if classes and workshops on character were included as mandatory curriculum in public and private schools? I am sure it would play a role in reducing dropout rates, and improving academic results and lifestyles.

ON MARRIAGE FAILURES: Divorce is a hazard of weak character. If you lack patience and persistence, you are in danger of losing your commitment (a character strength) to sticking it out in your marriage through thick and thin, which, in turn, can lower the quality of your family's lives. Today, about thirty-five percent of all marriages end up on the rocks—an unacceptable epidemic. (Some statistics are far higher). Broken families have profound effects on our children. If everyone had patience, persistence, and commitment, these problems would become virtually non-existent. Some divorces may be justified because of abuse or infidelity. But even abuse and infidelity are results of weak character.

SUBSTANCE ABUSE: Alcohol-related deaths are results of weak character. Twenty-five thousand people die in America each year because of drunk-driving-related accidents, and many times that number are injured. These are higher statistics than deaths resulting from some of the wars we have fought. If these drivers had self-control these statistics wouldn't exist. And consider the other statistics of ruined health such as cirrhosis of the liver, diabetes, lost jobs, damaged careers, ruined marriages, and broken families. Again, it's not an exaggeration that weak character can ruin and destroy lives. The social cost of weak character is far higher than we realize. Can you now see how important strong character is for our well-being, as well as for the well-being of others?

SMOKING-RELATED DEATHS: According to the Centers for Disease Control, smoking-related deaths amount to 440,000 people dying annually in America. These statistics become real when we realize that deaths from cancer and emphysema alone are *well over 500 times* the total American casualty rate, in the six-year Iraqi war, of over 4,300 military deaths, as of the end of 2009. Lack of self-control takes it toll.

REGARDING OTHER DEATHS AND DISEASES: Over-dosing, sexually transmitted diseases, cardio-vascular diseases, cancer, diabetes, high blood pressure, stroke, obesity, and the like are mainly due to lack of self-control, as manifested in what we eat, drink, smoke, snort, and inject, and further complicated by unhealthy and sedentary lifestyles. Adding to the mix of causes, Americans consume far too much sugar, salt, fried foods, processed foods, fatty foods, foods with artificial ingredients, junk foods, and so on, all because of a lack of self-control and a widespread ignorance of nutrition. Wouldn't it be great if basic nutrition were made a mandatory subject in our schools? If this were the case, many of the people you and I knew who died early would still be with us.

WITH REGARDS TO ABORTION: According to the latest statistics available, by the National Right to Life Committee, approximately 3,300 babies have been aborted each *day*—roughly equaling seventy-five percent of the total number of our soldiers killed in the Iraqi war in its first *six years*, and, in fact, *exceeds* the casualty rate of *every other war* we have ever fought. Why? It is because of the lack of self-control, self-denial, and because many people do not want the responsibilities that accompany raising children. Not taking responsibility is another character weakness, because it requires work, inconvenience, expense, and sacrifice, all of which would have otherwise paid much richer dividends later.

THE ISSUES OF UNEMPLOYMENT, POVERTY, AND HOMELESSNESS: Unemployment and poverty are *usually* results of weak character, due to a lack of persistence, patience, or preparation for the future. As indicated above, every man needs to learn how to do something, whether it be a trade, a skill, or a profession, so that when he finishes school, he can better provide for himself and his family. By knowing how to do something meaningful, he will not have to beg, steal, sell drugs to survive, or become a ward of the state, or do drugs as an escape from his miseries. The more you learn, the more you earn.

Pastor Thurman Scrivner, of the Living Savior Ministries, in Justin, Texas, said his father told him when he was a boy, "Son, whatever you do, when you go out into the world, don't put all your eggs into one basket. Don't go to work for, say, General Motors and put bumpers on cars for ten years and then they decide they don't need you, and you get out, and you don't know how to do anything. It might be hard to find somebody that needs a bumper on the front end of a car." So he said, "Do a lot of different things. That way, by doing a lot of things, if one job plays out, you'll have something else you'll fall back on." Thurman took that advice and learned to do "a lot of things," which has played a role to his leading an incredibly full, useful life. Yes, "knowledge is power." *The heart of the prudent getteth knowledge; and the ear of the wise seeketh knowledge. (Proverbs 18:15).*

When you apply for a job, the first thing an employer wants to know is, "What you can do?" If you don't have a skill, you'll walk away without a job. The best you could hope for is getting an unskilled job somewhere else. I've often thought of making bumper stickers saying, "FIGHT POVERTY. LEARN HOW TO DO SOMETHING."

It takes persistence, patience, and work to prepare for survival and life. Do not believe otherwise. I have a poster in my office regarding persistence, which says:

> "Press On
> Nothing in the world can take the place of persistence. Talent will not;
> Nothing is more common than unsuccessful men with talent.
> Genius will not; unrewarded genius is almost a proverb.
> Education alone will not; the world is full of educated derelicts.
> Persistence and determination alone are omnipotent." (*President Calvin Coolidge*).

The above statement is an overstatement pertaining to persistence as being "omnipotent," because only God is omnipotent. But it makes the point by hyperbole. Persistence, patience, and preparation for the future—by education and learning how to do things—are good ways to avoid unemployment, poverty, homelessness, and the other the pitfalls in life.

WITH REGARDS TO TELEVISION: Excessive television-watching as an escape, and the biggest activity-robber of all, is a hazard of weak character—and further perpetuates weak character. We cannot develop character—or anything else—by sitting and watching others do things while we do nothing. "TV-aholics"—and there are *tens* of millions of them—become lazy over time (one of the worst character weaknesses) and impatient (another character weakness), and become fat, weak, and unrealistic in the process, all of which further erodes our character and our quality of life, over time. Someone once wrote on a sidewalk near my home, "Turn off your TV and live!" I say "Amen" to that! Wouldn't you agree? You are infinitely better off with reading, radio, and CD's—which require at least some imagination to picture what is being read and said, and this helps to exercise and develop the imagination. Conversely, television develops nothing, not to mention the harmful and negative influences it has.

With regards to reading as being one antidote to television, I would like to relate to you here a story on how reading helped change Doctor Ben Carson's life and propelled him to success. When Ben was in the fifth grade, he was failing in most of his subjects. His mother, Sonya, knew that Ben and his brother, Curtis, were bright and had great potential. Sonya told the boys,

> If you keep making grades like this, you'll spend the rest of your life sweeping floors in a factory. And that's not what God wants for you.
>
> Sonya pulled Ben and Curtis close to her and looked right into their faces. "Boys, I don't know what to do. But God promises in the Bible to give wisdom to those who ask. So tonight I'm going to pray for wisdom. I'm going to ask God what I need to do to help you."
>
> Ben and Curtis didn't know what to think about their mother's words. Had she gone off the deep end? Did she

really think God was going to tell her how to help them get better grades?

Two days later, the boys found out God's answer to their mother's prayer, and they didn't like it. "God says we need to turn off the television," Sonya told her sons. "You may choose three television shows a week, but three times per week is it. You can use the extra time for reading."

The boys complained and tried to change her mind, but their mother wasn't finished. "You're also to write two book reports every week about what you read. Then you can present your reports out loud to me."

God's answer didn't seem very wise to Ben or Curtis. But they did as their mother said. They turned off the television, walked to the nearest branch of the Detroit Public Library, and checked out a stack of books.

Some of the people thought Ben's mother was being too hard on her sons. Several of her friends talked to her, telling her the boys needed more time to play outside. They warned her that Curtis and Ben would hate her for making them turn off the TV to read books and write reports.

But those people were wrong. Ben never hated his mother. Yes, he told her she was making them work too hard. But inside he knew she loved him and Curtis, and only wanted the best for them. Ben believed her when she said that if he tried, he could anything he wanted to do.

Sonya was tough and demanding...

She had high expectations for Curtis and Ben, and she never let them forget it. She observed the lives and habits of the successful people and wealthy people whose homes she cleaned every day. "They are no different from us," she told her sons. "Anything they can do, you can do. And if you really want to and you work hard, you can do it better."

In Sonya's mind, education would be the key to her sons' success. When other parents questioned the demands she placed on Curtis and Ben, she would tell them, "Say what you want, but my boys are going to be something. They're going to be self-supporting and learn how to love other folks. And no matter what they decide to do, they're going to be the best in the world at it."

The boys were grateful their mother hadn't said *what* they had to read. That meant they were free to choose books that interested them. Ben loved animals. So he read all the animal books he could find, then moved on to plants and rocks.

The Carson's lived near railroad tracts. Soon, Ben found himself collecting rocks in little boxes and taking them home to look up in his library books. Before long, he could identify almost any rock he found. He was proud of himself, but he thought it wise not to mention his new hobby to anyone at school.

One day Mr. Jaeck, Ben's science teacher, walked into his fifth-grade classroom with a big, shiny black rock. He held it up and asked, "Can anyone tell me what this is?"

Ben waited for one of the smart kids to answer. No one did. So he waited for one of the dumb kids to respond. More silence. Finally, Ben's hand went up. And as it did, his classmates began to whisper and giggle. "Hey, look," someone said. "Carson has his hand up! This oughta be good!"

Mr. Jaeck was surprised too. "Benjamin?"

"That's obsidian." Ben answered. Suddenly, the classroom was quiet. It sounded good. But no one was sure if it was the right answer—or a joke.

"That's right! It *is* obsidian," Mr. Jaeck exclaimed.

No one else was saying anything, so Ben continued: "Obsidian is formed after a volcanic eruption. Lave flows down and when it hits water, there is a supercooling process. The elements mix together, forcing out the air. Then the surface glazes."

"Right again, Benjamin!" Mr. Jaeck remarked with excitement in his voice. "Class, this is a tremendous piece of information Benjamin has just given us. I'm proud of him." Before he went on with his lesion, Mr. Jaeck asked Ben to stop by after school. His teacher wanted to work on Ben's rock collection with him.

Everyone stared at Ben in astonishment. But the most surprised person in the room was Ben himself. For the first time, he realized that he was not a dummy after all!

Ben also realized that he had known the answer because he'd been reading books. As that sank in, he began to wonder, *What if I read books about all of my subjects? Maybe I would know more than anyone in the class—more than the kids who tease me and call me names!*

Ben had made a giant discovery. But he couldn't yet imagine how much reading would change his life. The truth was he had found the key that would unlock his future and someday enable his greatest dreams to come true.[2]

Earlier in his life, when Ben was eight years old, he became inspired by reading another book to become a doctor. Ben ultimately went on to become a world-famous pediatric neurosurgeon.

Many people have been inspired to greatness by reading, but I have never heard of anyone becoming inspired to greatness from watching television.

---

[2] Taken from portions of Chapter three, originally published as: *Gifted Hands: The Ben Carson Story*, by Gregg Lewis and Deborah Shaw Lewis. Copyright © 2009 by Zonderkidz.

Have you? Do you know any successful "couch potatoes?

Abraham Lincoln said, "My best friend is the man who'll get me a book I ain't read."

Ben's mother, who cleaned homes for a living, noticed that the wealthy people she worked for did not spend much time watching television.

Many murders, crimes, perversions, bad habits, and bad live styles have been instilled into millions of kids and adults by years of doing nothing but watching television. And we wonder why the crime rate is ever increasing, along with drugs, perversions, abortions, divorces, sicknesses, and unhealthy lifestyles. The A. C. Nielson rating company's latest data shows that the average television viewer watches more than 151 hours of television per month, equaling about thirty-five hours a week, almost equivalent to that of a typical work week. The average child or teen watches nearly three hours of television a day, according to the Nutrition Health Center in Chesterton, Indiana. Wouldn't they be better off reading, playing outside, sports, or working? Wouldn't it be great if every neighborhood had a park or some open space, or gym, or at least something within reasonable *walking* distances of their homes, where kids and adults could go and play basketball, baseball, or just let loose? That is what I would call "better-planned communities." Some old houses and buildings might need to be torn down to make space for ball fields, basketball courts, swimming pools, gyms, and playgrounds for people of all ages to get together and have fun, live better lives, and further boost their strength of character while boosting their strength. Is it expensive? Yes. But the alternative is more expensive—in social costs to society, and in the form of plagues that would otherwise accompany character weaknesses.

Television is also a conversation-robber, thereby contributing to marriage failures and weakened relationships or no relationships due to lack of sufficient communication between a husband and a wife and family members, neighbors and acquaintances. Some people who watch television day and night are actually socially isolated because they learn to "relate" to the television more than they relate to people.

Television has, for all practical purposes, become an idol, particularly in America. Bill Britt, a successful businessman from North Carolina once said, "If every television in set America were destroyed, America would be instantly improved!" I basically agree. But there are some good uses of television such as Christian programming, educational channels, and balanced news. However, the negative effects of television far outweigh any limited beneficial effects it may have. It is just entertainment primarily, and we get more than enough entertainment as it is.

Television is even more harmful to children, because they are at the moldable, impressionable age, and unaware of what is happening to them. Kids need to be outside playing instead of watching television for hours every day. It's probably alright for them to watch some TV at night, but in the daytime, keep your kids busy. Get them out of the house, by turning off the television, when the weather is reasonably good. They will also make more friends outside than they will by staying inside—unless, of course, they are afflicted with physical issues which may prevent them from spending much time outside. But, assuming they are reasonably healthy, get them involved in sports. Play ball with them. Take them fishing. By spending more time outside, they will develop better social skills, motor skills, sharing skills, and give-and-take skills. They will learn more about life and things, all of which will gradually but surely add to their character, as well as their overall development. Steer clear of the tube, yourself, to set an example.

Encourage them to do things. Teach them to work and to help around the house, if necessary. Get involved with their education. When you take an interest in them, their teachers will take more of an interest in them. Spend time with them. They need you to do that, whether they know it of not. Once I saw a bumper sticker that said, "Spend time with your kid now so he won't have to do time later." Actually it is not so much as "spending" time with your kids, as it is in "investing" time with them. It stands to reason that the more time you take with your kids the better lives they will have, and you will have also.

Finally, I suspect there is a connection with excessive television watching and Alzheimer's disease. It stands to reason that if excessive television watching weakens the imagination it must weaken the mind as a whole. Middle-aged, retired, and elderly people are particularly vulnerable because most, or at least many, of them are predictably less active, further compounded by the fact that they spend inordinate amounts to time watching television day and night. I would also suspect that the incidence of Alzheimer's disease in America is more prevalent than in most of the rest of the world, because virtually every home here has at least one or more television sets. In the developing countries there are far fewer television sets per capita, and the people are more active.

There is a report in the Proceedings of the National Academy of Sciences of a study initiated in 1991 of 193 patients who either possibly or probably had Alzheimer's and 358 of their healthy friends, neighbors or acquaintances. Name of the report: *Patients With Alzheimer's Disease Have Reduced Activities in Midlife Compared With Healthy Control-group Members.* In the study it was found that Alzheimer's is associated with reduced activities, and that odds ratios showed that people who were relatively inactive (for intellectual, passive, or physical activities) had about a 250 per cent increased risk of developing Alzheimer's. The report stated that under activity is a risk factor for the development of Alzheimer's.

Inactivity is worse. With few exceptions, *no* activity is involved in television watching. I am not aware of any more recent studies of the link between television and Alzheimer's or dementia in general. But I think the matter is well worth further looking into, because the disease is becoming more and more common. Excessive television watching is indeed a "vegetater."

After all, if God told Ben Carson's mother, Sonya, to "turn off the television" wouldn't you agree, that God is telling us to turn off the television, and that we will likewise benefit, by at least cutting it back to a few shows a week? Is God ever wrong?

THE MATTER OF DEBT: Excessive debt is a hazard of weak character. Most people are in debt of one kind or another. Most companies are in debt. Most churches are in debt. The government is hopelessly in debt. We used to be a creditor nation, lending and giving to other countries. Now, because of so many people, companies, organizations, and the government borrowing like drunken sailors for decades, we have now become the world's largest debtor nation, now owing to other countries. I believe that a *high* percentage of Americans have become what I'll call "borrowaholics," – an unrecognized, undiagnosed addiction that is epidemic among us. Most of us don't want to wait until we can afford it. So we been borrowing to "get it now," thereby paying some twenty to twenty-five percent more than the purchase prices and gradually bringing us ever deeper into debt, which has to be paid back.

Why are so many people drowning in debt? It is because of the lack of patience, self-control, self-discipline, and self-denial, and I might add the desire "to keep up with the Joneses." We've become the "I want it now—instant gratification" generation. The Bible warns us about debt. *Owe no man any thing, but to love one another. (Romans 13:8).* And *The borrower is servant to the lender. (Proverbs 22:7).* Do what the Bible says, and pay as you go. Get out of debt, and stay out of debt. Of course, the purchase of homes and cars usually requires going into debt, because very few people have enough money to buy such items up front with cash. But the misuse of credit cards and other loans need to be avoided, except in emergencies.

CHARACTER LEVELS AS A POLITICAL FACTOR: Another hazard of weak character is if the overall "character index" of a people is low, they tend to elect politicians whose caliber is likewise low. After God, the overall character index of our people determines the character of our elected leaders. People with strong character tend to vote for *statesmen* who make hard decisions based on peoples' *needs*, whereas people with weak character tend to vote for *politicians* who make promises to the people according to their *wants* rather than their needs.

One reason so many of our elected government officials are short-sighted and choose the easy but wrong paths is because elected officials are often reflections of the people who elect them, while others in the electorate are apathetic, uninformed, or misinformed. Too many people want the government to take care of them. They lack independence (a character trait). They want the government to provide them with welfare, healthcare, public housing, food stamps, handouts, increased minimum wages, etc., at the expense of everyone else and in the form of ever-increasing taxes, at the expense of everyone who works. So we end up with weak leaders, because so many people are weak in character.

As H. L. Mencken once said, "We get the government we deserve." So it's not an overstatement to say that character is important at all levels of our society.

I don't like criticizing, judging, and being negative. It goes against my grain. But there is a problem, and somebody needs to address it, because we all have more potential than we have realized. Most of us can provide for ourselves far better than government can. The present system of government handouts and creeping socialism isn't working, is it? Has socialism or Marxism ever worked anywhere? Is there a socialist country you would like to move to? Of course not. Their people would love to move here, and many of them have.

Socialism works beautifully, in theory only. It has never worked in actuality, anywhere. It never will. You would think we would have learned by now, by just observing. Are you aware of any socialist country that is prospering? I'm not. Socialism weakens the rich and the poor alike while trying to create the "Utopia" of a classless society. Under socialism, et al, lives and economies have been ruined. And, yes, socialism weakens and ruins the character of its people by making the people ever more dependent upon the government. With socialism, we end up with a strong government and a weak people. Be smart. Look at the *results* of socialism and Marxism—not at the theories.

Almost every ill we have as a country can be traced back in some way, in whole or in part, to the role that weak character plays in the low overall "character index" of the people. Do I have an agenda? Yes! I have a bunch of them. But I am not picking on anyone, because virtually all of us have character weaknesses, to varying degrees.

CHARACTER WEAKNESSES, A HAZARD OF CIVILIZATION: At this point, I might add that civilization itself has been part of the problem. Civilization is not a hazard of weak character; but rather weak character is a hazard of civilization. I'm not advocating going back to the "stone age" days, of course. But if we are smart enough to create a civilization, we can certainly be smart enough to figure out how we can remedy the hazards that civilization poses to character. A glut of conveniences, luxuries, entertainments, and the easy life spawned by civilization have added to making most of us soft, lazy, sedentary, and, hence, weaker in character. Each succeeding generation gets "softer" than the previous generation. The body is made for action; and, "if we don't use it we lose it." Someone once aptly said, "This generation has been weakened by the ignorance of adversity." However, we can solve the problem because we are now beginning to understand that the problem exists, and its solutions.

Study Guide —Chapter 5

Try coming up with the answers on your own, as a mental exercise, before looking them up:

1. What are some hazards of the lack of self-control? Pg. 61.

2. What are some hazards of the lack of patience? Pgs. 61–63.

3. What are some other hazards of weak character? Pgs. 63–68.

4. How can excessive television watching weaken character? Pg. 68.

5. How can excessive television watching weaken the imagination? Pg. 68.

6. When Dr. Ben Carson was a boy, his mother recognized that excessive television watching was causing problems in his and his brother's learning abilities. What was their mother's solution to the problem? And what resulted from the solution? What was Ben's "giant discovery" to the solution to the problem, and how did it affect his entire life? Pgs. 68–71.

7. What did Ben's mother, who cleaned homes for a living, notice about the wealthy people she worked for? Pg. 72.

8. How has television contributed to weakened marriages and relationships in general? Pg. 73.

9. Television has, for all practical purposes, become an _____ to many. Pg. 73.

10. A report in the proceedings of the National Academy of Sciences stated that under activity is a risk factor for the development of ___________. Pg. 75.

11. Why are so many people swimming in debt? Pgs. 76 & 77.

12. Politicians of low caliber are ordinarily elected by people of ______ character. Pgs. 77 & 78.

13. How can character weaknesses be a hazard of civilization? Pgs. 79 & 80.

Chapter 6

The Bible speaks

Are there Bible scriptures that speak to us regarding this matter of character? I'm glad you asked. Here are some of them:

Proverbs 6:6-11 (regarding laziness)—*Go to the ant, thou sluggard; consider her ways, and be wise: Which having no guide, overseer, or ruler, Provideth her meat in the summer, and gathereth her food in the harvest. How long wilt thou sleep, O sluggard? When wilt thou arise out of thy sleep? Yet a little sleep, a little slumber, a little folding of the hands to sleep: So shall thy poverty come as one that travelleth, and thy want as an armed man.*

Proverbs 10:4-5—*He becometh poor that dealeth with a slack hand: but the diligent maketh rich. He that gathereth in summer is a wise son: but he that sleepeth in harvest is a son that causeth shame.*

Proverbs 17:3—*The refining pot is for silver, and the furnace for gold: but the Lord trieth the hearts.* (In other words, God strengthens us through trials and tribulations).

Proverbs 18:9—*He that is slothful in his work is brother to him that is a great waster.*

Proverbs 19:15—*Slothfulness casteth into a deep sleep; and an idle soul shall suffer hunger.*

Proverbs 19:18—*Chasten thy son while there is still hope, and let not thy soul spare for his crying.*

Proverbs 20:4—*The sluggard will not plow by reason of the cold; therefore shall he beg in harvest, and have nothing.*

Proverbs 20:13—*Love not sleep, lest thou come to poverty; open thine eyes, and thou shalt be satisfied with bread.*

Proverbs 21:25—*The desire of the slothful killeth him; for his hands refuse to labor.*

Proverbs 23:21—*Drowsiness shall clothe a man with rags.*

Proverbs 24:33-34—*A little sleep, a little slumber, a little folding of the hands to sleep: So shall thy poverty come as one that travelleth; and thy want as an armed man.*

Proverbs 25:28—*He that hath no rule over his own spirit* (i.e. no self-control) *is like a city that is broken down, and without walls.*

Proverbs 31:27—*Eateth not the bread of idleness.*

Acts 20:35—*It is more blessed to give than to receive.* (As listed earlier, generosity is a character trait. Giving strengthens us.)

Romans 5:3-4—*We glory in tribulations also: knowing that tribulation worketh patience; And patience, experience; and experience, hope.*

Galatians 5:23—*Meekness* (i.e. humility), *temperance* (i.e. moderation): *against such there is no law.*

Galatians 6:5—*Every man shall bear his own burden.*

Ephesians 4:1-2—*Walk worthy of the vocation wherewith ye are called, With all lowliness and meekness, with longsuffering* (i.e. patience), *forbearing one another in love.*

Ephesians 4:28—*Let him that stole steal no more: but rather let him labour, working with his hands the thing which is good, that he may have to give to him that needeth.*

1 Thessalonians. 4:11—*Do your own business, and work with your own hands.*

2 Thessalonians 3:10—*If any would not work, neither should he eat.* (Work is a great developer of character).

Hebrews 12:5-6 & 11—*Despise not thou the chastening of the Lord, nor faint when thou art rebuked of him: For whom the Lord loveth he chasteneth, and scourgeth every son he receiveth...Now no chastening for the present seemeth to be joyous, but grevious: nevertheless afterward it yieldeth the peaceable fruit of righteousness unto them which are exercised thereby.*

James 1:2-4—*Count it all joy when ye shall fall into divers temptations; Knowing this, that the trying of your faith worketh patience. But let patience have her perfect work, that ye may be perfect and entire, wanting nothing.* (Resisting temptations requires self-control, which, in turn, develops patience.)

1 Peter 5:10—*The God of all grace, who hath called us unto His eternal glory by Christ Jesus, after that ye have suffered a while, make you perfect, stablish, strengthen, settle you.*

2 Peter 1:5-7—*Giving all diligence, add to your faith virtue; and to virtue knowledge; And to knowledge temperance; and to temperance patience; and to patience godliness; And to godliness brotherly kindness; and to brotherly kindness charity* (i.e. love).

The Word is peppered throughout with other scriptures regarding goodness, righteousness and related character traits.

People with strong character appreciate the value of relationships, money and material things; and they maintain these things. They are good stewards of what God has given them.	**People with weak character** do not appreciate or understand the value of relationships, money and material things, and they do little or nothing to maintain these things. If I am speaking about you, you can change!
People with strong character hear and believe what they *need* to hear and believe. For example, when they hear constructive criticism or warnings, they accept it and do something about it.	**People with weak character** tend to hear and believe only what they *want* to hear and believe. When they hear constructive criticism or warnings, they are normally offended, and usually do nothing about it.
People with strong character are doers.	**People with weak character** are more talkers than doers.
People with strong character think of the future. They see the big picture. Therefore, they prepare, work, and	**People with weak character** think of the present. They don't consider the big picture. So they do not prepare,

sacrifice for the future. (Again, every man needs to learn a trade, a profession or a skill to prepare for life, to adequately provide for his family, and be useful to his community.)

work and sacrifice for the future because of laziness (perhaps the biggest character weakness). Rather than learning a trade, profession, or a skill to prepare for life, they do what they *want* to do for the moment rather than doing what they *need* to do for the future. Consequently, they never end up having reached their full potentials; they don't earn as much as they otherwise would have and end up living sub-standard shortened lives, and some of them become homeless. They seek to satisfy their appetites for the moment with sex, drugs, alcohol, excessive eating, or just vegetating in front of the television—anything that feels good, entertains, or provides an escape. Lacking foresight, they haven't been thinking of the long-term consequences of their actions and inactions. They are "pleasure seekers." They've sacrificed the future for the pleasures of the present. *He that loveth pleasure shall be a poor man. (Proverbs. 21:17).* Aren't these Bible scriptures accurate and relevant?

"Preaching" is not necessary here, except to say that we can all agree on the consequences and complications of the fruits of excessive pleasure seeking—such as unwanted pregnancies, diseases, addictions, ruined careers, poverty, broken families, and failures—and what these things do to people, their families, careers, and lives... If you fall into this category, there is still hope for you. With God, there is no such thing as a hopeless person. You are not a hopeless person. If you do not give up on yourself, God will not give up on you. If God can raise the dead, He can certainly raise you up, with your obedience, of course. If you think I am judging you, I'm not. The late jazz singer, Ella Fitzgerald, said, "God don't make no junk." If you've been wallowing in the junk, you can get out of it. But, you can't do it without God, so turn to Him, and get going! You can do it. Jesus is your answer. After all, He did say, *I am the way.* (John 14:6) What other answer is there? He put His money where His mouth is, and literally died for you.

***

When a man has character he has strength. And the more character he has the more strength he has, and the more of a *man* he is.

If a man has little character then he is weak. He is more of a *male* than a man. Examples include a deadbeat dad, an abusive husband, an abusive father, or he is not the real head of the household. If you fall into this category, again I say you can get out of it with God's help.

If a man is devoid of character, then he becomes a *monster* and not a man. Examples include a serial killer, sex-offender, and sadist. Wouldn't you agree? If you are devoid of character, Jesus can still set you free. *If the Son therefore shall make you free, ye shall be free indeed. (John 8:36).*

***

Weak character can lead to and contribute to other problems such as low self-image, mid-life crisis, social isolation, depression, failure in general, and suicide. One thing can lead to and feed on another, akin to the domino effect. Again, weak character has ultimately ruined lives. To restate, the best antidote to the problem of weak character is simply that of activities—to work, to get busy, exercise, study, and prepare. One reason that *activity* is of paramount importance is because it is stimulating, and it is stimulation that produces growth in anything, including the growth in character. Our bodies are made for action. We are made for action. So, turn off the television and do something. Get moving. Start, now, even if it is something small. But if you're going to start "later," it's a safe bet that you won't start at all. Remember, "If you don't use it you lose it." So don't vegetate. Activate. Do something each day—maybe just one thing each day—until you start getting somewhere. Then, keep on going, and gradually step it up. Grab a hold of yourself, and make yourself do what you should do. Take control of yourself. You're the "captain" of your life. *Nobody* is going to do it for you. So do not let your body tell you what to do. You tell your body what to do, like Paul did. Paul wrote *Fight I, not as one that beateth the air: But I keep my body, and bring it into subjection. (1 Corinthians 9:26-27).* Paul told his body what to do. He did not let his body tell him what to do. So, because Paul didn't give in to the flesh, and because of his self-discipline and self-control, God accomplished great things through him.

By now, I think you would agree that the predominant importance of character is evident. It is a subject that has never received much attention, because it has never been sufficiently understood. Weak character can hurt, destroy, and kill. It can lower one's quality of life. These assessments are not exaggerations. Instead, character weaknesses among us are widespread and unrecognized. All we have to do is look around and see the widespread fruits of weak character, namely:

- drugs
- alcoholism
- crime
- rape
- prostitution
- pornography
- perversions
- unhealthy lifestyles
- abortion
- gambling
- lying
- cheating
- sin in general
- homelessness
- diseases
- domestic violence
- child abuse
- child neglect
- dysfunctional families
- broken families
- people losing their homes
- bankruptcies, suicides
- virtually all the social problems

To be weak in character can destroy you in this life and in the next. Isn't that right? Avoid it!

Needless to say, Satan would love us all to be weak in character. He puts thoughts in our minds and in the minds of others, thoughts that can lead us to making mistakes and sin, which can lead to ruined lives. On the other hand, God speaks to us through the quiet still voice of His Holy Spirit to help us make the right decisions, which can lead us to strong character and abundant lives. We all hear from God and satan, in many different ways, including through thoughts and through some people. Because God gives us free will, our outcomes all depend on who we listen to.

Yet not all is lost. We are all born with the potential for great character. It still can be developed and strengthened with God's help. So, if you're not satisfied with where you are in life because of your level of character, and you want to improve, no matter what level your character is, you can do all things through Christ who strengthens you. *I can do all things through Christ which strengtheneth me. (Philippians 4:13)*; and God cannot lie. *God is not a man, that he should lie. (Numbers 23:19).* So...

Study Guide —Chapter 6

Try coming up with the answers on your own, as a mental exercise, before looking them up:

1. What are some Bible scriptures that speak to us regarding character? Pgs. 83–85.

2. What are some differences of people with strong character and people with weak character? Pgs. 86–88.

3. What are some differences between a *man*, a *male*, and a *monster*? Pg. 89.

4. What are some of the things that weak character leads to? Pgs. 89–91.

5. The best antidote to weak character is ________? Pgs. 89 & 90.

6. Don't let your body _____ you what to do. You _____ your body what to do. Pg. 90.

7. What are some of the "fruits" of weak character, such as drugs, rape, and so on? Pg. 91.

Chapter 7
Where Do We Go From Here?

Now I trust that you have some idea of what you may need to work on. We all need to work on things to varying degrees, don't we? It has been said that good habits are hard to get and easy to lose, and conversely, bad habits are easy to get and hard to get rid of. So expect a battle. But anything that is hard is worth fighting for. The rewards will far exceed the struggle. When you do something for twenty-one straight days without missing a day, you've developed a habit. However, if you miss a day before you reach day twenty-one, start over again from day one; and keep at it until you reach twenty-one consecutive days. Then it becomes a habit and is no longer a "pain" to do. It becomes routine or second nature. Stick with it and then work on any other habit(s) you want to develop or get rid of. Every good habit you have and develop adds to your character, and every bad habit you get rid of likewise strengthens your character. You probably already know what habits you need to make or break.

The subject of character is so important, I have no doubt that, *after* God, strong character is the most important success factor in life, because it encompasses so many traits. The more you strengthen your character the more of your potential you will fulfill. So, do you want to reach your full potential? Strengthen your character. The matter of character—strong or weak—is a salient underlying critical factor in every society. Character plays a role in everything we do and don't do. It's just the way we are wired. In fact, the study of character is like a virtual study of life, because so many of the issues that pertain to character pertain to life.

Study Guide —Chapter 7

Try coming up with the answers on your own, as a mental exercise, before looking them up:

1. Every good habit you have and make adds to your ___________, and every bad habit you break likewise ___________ your character. Pg. 95.

2. Character plays a role in ___________ we do and don't do, except sleep. Pg. 96.

Chapter 8

Defining Character

Now that we have a better idea as to what character is, how we get character, and how we can strengthen character, we are now ready to define character. Because the subject of character is so in depth, it can be defined in three ways, in **bold**, as follows:

We all have abilities. However many of us do not have the ability to use our abilities. Why?

Many of us do not have the ability to use our abilities because of the character weaknesses of lack of self-control, lack of self-discipline, and/or laziness. So, most of us have not yet come even close to reaching our full potentials. Therefore, here is the main definition of character:

Character is doing what we should do, whether we feel like it or not.

Character is self-control. Earlier I made reference to "self-control" as being a "trait" of character.

However, the more I think about it, the more I am convinced that self-control encompasses all the other character traits. Therefore, self-control is character and character is self-control. They are one and the same.

Character is an accumulation of good habits. The more good habits we have, the more character we have; the fewer good habits we have, the less character we have.

As a sort of "footnote" to the above three *definitions* of character, I would like to add a *description* of character, as follows. If you don't feel like doing something that you should do, but you go ahead and do it anyway, that is character. However, if you don't feel like doing something that you should do, and you likewise do not do it that is laziness. Hence, the opposite of character is laziness (the worst character trait); and the opposite of laziness is character. Therefore, a lazy person is weak in character and is a candidate for failure in life, unless he gets rid of his laziness habit. Moreover, a person who is not lazy has strong character and is a good candidate for becoming successful in life.

Study Guide —Chapter 8

Try coming up with the answers on your own, as a mental exercise, before looking them up:

1. What is the main definition of character? Pg. 97.

2. The opposite of character is _________. Pg. 98.

Chapter 9

One Last Word

If you are not satisfied with where you are in life, it is mainly because you had a problem that you did not know that you had. In a nutshell, you have not been able to do what you are able to do. Why? You were more than likely weak in some of the character traits like persistence, patience, and self-control—the weaknesses of which are different forms of laziness. The solution: you have the ability. Now strengthen your character to use your abilities, as shown in this book, in the areas where you think you have been weak.

The younger you are when you build up your character, the less difficult it will be. Conversely, the older you are in developing your character, the more work will be required—the reason: as we age, we tend to become set in our ways and resistant to change. But you have no choice but to win in order to have a better, longer, fruitful life, and make a difference. I want that for you.

There is so much of all kinds of loss, sadness, and death in this world because of character weaknesses. I don't want that for you.

Therefore, If you have read this book rapidly or in one sitting, and you believe that the information contained herein is important, I would encourage you to go over this book again one or more times—whatever it takes—to reinforce what you have already learned, and to get it into your spirit. Read it a little at a time, in digestible "bites." Don't be in a hurry. Re-read a little of it each day so that it will be more easily remembered and assimilated. As you re-read this book, God will reinforce and reveal more things to you, as you are ready to receive them.

I don't care who you are, or what you are. I am pulling for you. I want you to overcome and succeed. I want you to have a better life and to bless others. As I was almost finished with this book, I was praying that you would be blessed, helped, profit, and learn from this book, and that God's will be done for you and for all those you can and will touch. As I was praying, I was surprised to find myself suddenly breaking down and crying like a baby. I guess it was the Holy Spirit crying through me. God bless you, brothers and sisters.

Study Guide —Chapter 9

Try coming up with the answers on your own, as a mental exercise, before looking them up:

If you are not satisfied with where you are in life, strengthen your ____________. Pg. 101.

Extra:

As we strengthen our character we become more like _________.

About the Author

Dan is a retired businessman. He was a self-employed founder and owner of his own recruiting firm—the Tech-Prof Employment Service, Inc.—specializing primarily in the recruitment and job placement of Engineering and Computer professionals. He has over thirty years of experience in the field. He is an Army veteran, served in Germany, and graduated from The Citadel Military College of SC, receiving a BSBA degree. Dan is widowed, and has two grown sons and four grandchildren. He currently resides in Baltimore.

Did You Enjoy this Book?

Then please spread the word to your pastors, family and friends, and talk-radio host.

Dan welcomes all opportunities to speak to your church, group, event, retreat, or wherever people are in need of his message.

Contact: danielddj@verizon.net

www.ingramcontent.com/pod-product-compliance
Lightning Source LLC
Chambersburg PA
CBHW031323040426
42443CB00005B/201

* 9 7 8 0 9 7 9 0 2 2 1 6 6 *